Where Is the Sahara Desert?

by Sarah Fabiny

illustrated by David Malan

Penguin Workshop

To my dad—SF

For Alice—DM

PENGUIN WORKSHOP
An imprint of Penguin Random House LLC, New York

First published in the United States of America by Penguin Workshop,
an imprint of Penguin Random House LLC, New York, 2023

Visit us online at penguinrandomhouse.com.

Library of Congress Cataloging-in-Publication Data is available.

Printed in the United States of America

ISBN 9780593520062 (paperback)   10 9 8 7 6 5 4 3 2 1 WOR
ISBN 9780593520079 (library binding)   10 9 8 7 6 5 4 3 2 1 WOR

Contents

Where Is the Sahara Desert?

Ancient Egypt was one of the greatest, most powerful, and most stable civilizations in the history of the world. It lasted for over three thousand years, from 3150 BCE to 30 BCE.

The ancient Egyptians invented many things that we still use today, including ways to construct buildings and irrigate land, paper and ink, clocks, the toothbrush and toothpaste, and even breath mints.

Irrigation system

While the kingdom of ancient Egypt was very strong, it wasn't nearly as large as other ancient civilizations, like the Greek or Roman empires.

The ancient Egyptians established their kingdom in the strip of land that ran alongside the Nile River in northeast Africa.

The Nile River provided water, food, and transportation for the citizens of the kingdom. But beyond the banks of the Nile River lay arid, or dry, land—the Sahara Desert. To the east, it stretched a few hundred miles to the Red Sea. To the west, it extended for thousands of miles, all the way to the Atlantic Ocean.

The Nile River

The Egyptians called the barren desert the "red land." Although no crops could be grown there, it was still important to the ancient Egyptians. The miles of hot sand separated and protected the kingdom from invading armies. It also provided the ancient Egyptians with valuable natural resources. They used the rock and stone for monumental structures such as the pyramids. Semiprecious stones, such as malachite and turquoise, were used in their beautiful jewelry. And metals, like copper and gold, were transformed into tools and jewelry.

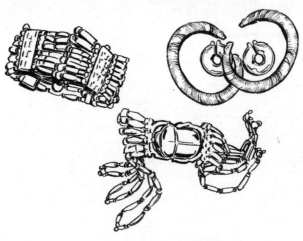

Ancient Egyptian jewelry

The ancient Egyptians could not live in the Sahara Desert. But they saw the miles and miles of this harsh landscape as an important and essential part of their lives and their civilization. The Sahara Desert is still as barren, dry, and arid as it was during the times of ancient Egypt. And it is still an important and essential part of our world.

CHAPTER 1
From Jungle to Desert

Imagine a place where you can walk for hundreds, even thousands, of miles and see only sand. A place that only gets a couple of inches of rainfall a year. That place exists, and it is the Sahara—the largest hot desert in the world. (Antarctica and the Arctic are larger deserts, but they are cold deserts.)

The Sahara is located in the northern part of the African continent. This huge desert lies within the Northern Hemisphere and runs through ten countries: Algeria, Chad, Egypt, Libya, Mali, Mauritania, Morocco, Niger, Sudan, and Tunisia, as well as a part of Africa known as Western Sahara. It extends more than three thousand miles from the Atlantic Ocean in the west to the Red Sea in

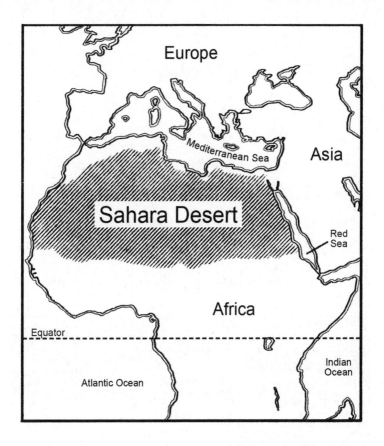

the east. It stretches over one thousand miles from
the Mediterranean Sea in the north to the Sahel
savanna in the south. (The Sahel savanna is an area
of grassland.) The Sahara covers a total of about
3.5 million square miles. That's approximately
the same size as the United States.

Say It Twice

"Sahara" comes from the Arabic word for desert: *sahra*. And this word is related to another word that describes the reddish color of the area. So when you say "Sahara Desert," you are actually saying "desert desert."

The Sahara Desert isn't the only place with a

name that repeats itself. *Tahoe* comes from a Native American word for "lake," so Lake Tahoe on the Nevada-California border means "lake lake." And "galaxy" comes from the ancient Greek word *galaxias*. The Greeks used this word, which means "milky," to describe a band of light they saw in the night sky. So when you say "Milky Way galaxy," you're actually saying "Milky Way milky."

Milky Way galaxy

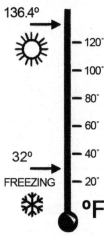

136.4°

32°

FREEZING

— 120°
— 100°
— 80°
— 60°
— 40°
— 20°

°F

On a summer day, the Sahara is among the hottest regions in the world. Temperatures often reach more than 120 degrees Fahrenheit. One of the hottest temperatures ever recorded on the planet was in the Sahara: In September 1922, the temperature hit 136.4 degrees Fahrenheit. That's hot enough to cook a steak to medium rare! But the temperature drops drastically at night. It can get very cold, and maybe even go below freezing in winter.

This vast desert is like a huge laboratory for scientists. They have studied and learned a lot about this region. But the one thing scientists have not been able to determine is exactly when the Sahara Desert was created. Some scientists think that the desert first appeared five to seven million years ago. During this time, some of the plates that make up the earth's surface collided and created the Alps. These mountains, along with the Himalayan mountains to the east, blocked winds that had once carried rain to the Sahara region. The area became very dry, and a desert was formed.

Himalayan mountains

Tectonic Plates

Slabs of rock called tectonic plates make up the earth's outer shell and fit together like a gigantic jigsaw puzzle. They sit on top of the hot inner layers of the earth and slowly shift around on this melted layer. Even though the plates only move one or two inches a year, they bump into one another all the time. Their movement causes earthquakes, tsunamis, and the eruption of volcanoes.

Other scientists believe the Sahara was originally formed around two to three million years ago during one of the ice ages that occurred on our planet. During this time, less rain fell on certain areas, including the Sahara region. As a result, the area dried out and eventually became a desert. And there are some scientists who suggest the Sahara first appeared during the last ice age, only tens of thousands of years ago. They believe that up until that time, this area always had a moist climate.

Scientists don't agree on when the Sahara Desert was first formed. But most agree that this dry, hot place was actually lush and green only about four thousand years ago. It was full of animal and plant life.

These scientists believe that the Sahara's climate switches back and forth about every twenty thousand years. It goes from a dry climate to a wet climate that allows plants and animals to thrive.

And right now, the Sahara is in the desert phase. Scientists think that about eleven thousand years ago, monsoon rains came to this region in Africa.

The area was covered with lakes, rivers, grasslands, and even forests. All kinds of animals lived in this green area. Hippos, giraffes, and elephants grazed in the grasslands, and fish and crocodiles swam in the rivers and lakes. It certainly would have looked very different than it does now.

But what caused this drastic change? It's believed that the earth tilted slightly on its axis about eleven thousand years ago. This tilting meant that the Northern Hemisphere was slightly closer to the sun, which increased the amount of rain brought to the region.

But then, about eight thousand years ago, the earth tilted on its axis again. So the Northern Hemisphere was a bit farther away from the sun. It received less summer sunlight and less rain, so the region of the Sahara began to dry up. What was once green became arid and dusty.

There are some scientists who believe that human beings and their livestock were also part of the reason for the change in the Sahara's landscape back then. People moved farther into the area and brought their animals with them. The animals, such as cows and goats, grazed on the grass and plants. The area was already drying out, but now there were fewer plants to hold the

moisture and soil in place. The ground dried out
and the dry soil blew away. What was once the
lush green Sahara became the Sahara Desert in
just a few hundred years.

A Tilting Planet

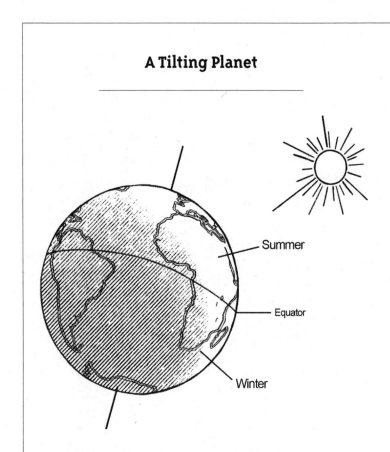

Summer

Equator

Winter

Rather than "sitting up straight," the earth is tilted on an axis. (The earth's axis is the imaginary line that runs through the center of the planet. One end of the axis is the North Pole and the other end is the South Pole.) And it's this tilt that gives us the seasons as the earth rotates on its axis and orbits the sun.

For half the year, the earth is tilted so that the North Pole is closer to the sun. For the other half, the South Pole is closer to the sun. When the North Pole is angled toward the sun, it's summer in the Northern Hemisphere (the part of the planet north of the equator). There's more sunlight, and the days are longer and nights are shorter. As the year progresses, the tilt of the earth changes. The North Pole is farther from the sun, which brings winter to the Northern Hemisphere.

Pictures Tell a Story

One of the reasons that we know that the Sahara had a very different climate is because of paintings and rock carvings, known as petroglyphs (say: peh-tro-glifs). Many of these paintings and petroglyphs are in Algeria and Sudan. They show images of crocodiles, hippopotamuses, giraffes, elephants, and other animals. They also show people with cattle, people hunting, and people fishing in boats. Thanks to these images, we have a record of what life was like for the earliest inhabitants of this region.

CHAPTER 2
Much More Than Sand

When you think of the Sahara Desert, you probably think of sand, sand, and more sand. But only about 15 to 20 percent of this desert is covered with sand dunes (hills). The rest is made up of other geographical landforms, from mountains to dry riverbeds.

1000 ft

The Sahara's sand dunes are mainly found in the desert's north central region, in the countries of Algeria and Libya. In some places, these dunes can reach as high as one thousand feet. That's about as tall as a one-hundred-story building! These massive sand structures are shaped by wind and gravity.

Sand dunes are masses of loose sand. The wind blows this sand up the back side, or back slope, until the grains of sand reach the top, or crest. Then, due to gravity, the sand drops down into the sheltered side of the dune that's not exposed to the wind. More sand is blown up and over, burying the sand blown before. As the wind continues to blow the sand, the sand dune moves across the landscape. This means that sand dunes are always moving and shifting. These areas of shifting sand dunes are called ergs.

Ergs as seen from above

Regs

Regs are huge plains of sand and gravel, which look a bit like the surface of the moon. This type of landform covers most of the Sahara, about 70 percent. Regs are the remains of prehistoric seabeds and riverbeds, and the gravel can be red, black, or white.

Hamadas (say: ha-MAH-das) also make up a large part of the Sahara Desert. In Arabic, *hamada* means "desert pavement." In these areas, the wind has blown away soil, sand, and dust. What's left are rocky plateaus (say: pla-tows). A plateau is a flat, raised area of land.

Hamadas

Singing Sands

Did you know that the sand in the Sahara sings? As grains of sand slide down the slopes of sand dunes, they make a deep hum that can be heard for miles. The singing sands often sound like the cellos in an orchestra warming up. But they can make a number of sounds. Scientists have discovered that deep within the dune is a very hard layer of sand. The sound that bounces off this layer is louder.

Marco Polo

These singing sand dunes can be heard in the Sahara, Mojave, and Gobi Deserts. When explorer Marco Polo heard the singing sand as he crossed the Gobi, he believed the sounds were the voices of mysterious spirits.

Found mainly in the northern Sahara, chotts (say: shots) are shallow salt lakes. While they're dry for most of the year, they do fill up in the winter when rainfall arrives. Some scenes from *Star Wars* were filmed in a large chott called Chott el Jerid in Tunisia.

Chott el Jerid

Deserts of the World

Deserts are found on every continent. Deserts actually cover about one-fourth of the earth's land. Each one is unique. But they all have one thing in common—they receive less than ten inches of rainfall a year. Here are some of the deserts found on our planet:

- **THE ATACAMA:** This desert stretches for six hundred miles along the west coast of South America. After Antarctica it is the driest place on Earth. It only gets about 0.04 inches of rain a year.

- **THE ARABIAN:** This desert makes up almost all of the Arabian Peninsula in the Middle East. The world's largest area of unbroken sand is found in this desert, and it also has places known for dangerous quicksand.

- **THE GOBI:** This desert stretches across parts of

northwest China and southern Mongolia. Many dinosaur fossils, including dinosaur eggs, have been found in the region.

The Gobi Desert

CHAPTER 3
Water in the Sahara

Even though the Sahara Desert hardly receives any rainfall, there is water in this vast sea of sand. Two of the world's largest rivers, the Nile and the Niger, actually flow through parts of the Sahara. The Nile, the longest river in the world, starts in eastern Africa, just south of the Sahara. It flows north through Sudan and Egypt and empties into the Mediterranean Sea. The Niger River, which is about 2,600 miles long, begins in western Africa. From there, the river flows northeast, through part of the Sahara Desert. But then it makes a bit of a U-turn and heads southeast. The Niger River empties into the Gulf of Guinea along the coast of Nigeria. Although the rivers are surrounded by desert in places,

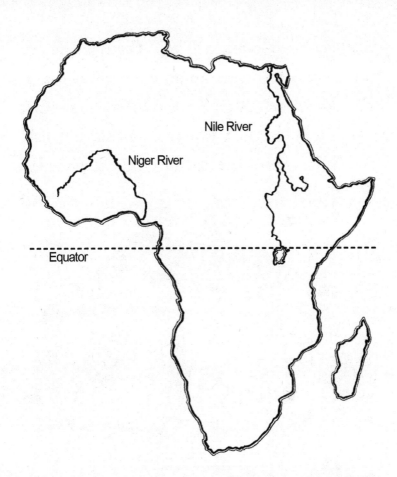

many people live along them and rely on the resources they provide.

In addition to these two great rivers, there is a group of eighteen lakes in the Sahara Desert. They are known as the Ounianga (say: on-ee-ang-ah) lakes and are located in Chad. The lakes vary in color, size, and depth. Some are freshwater lakes and some are saltwater lakes. The freshwater lakes are home to a variety of plants and fish. Since this area of the Sahara Desert receives less

than 0.08 inches of rain a year, the fact that there are lakes here at all is a natural wonder. Because of that they have been designated a World Heritage Site by the United Nations, meaning they have "outstanding universal value."

Ounianga lakes

The Biggest Lake in the World

Lake Chad is a freshwater lake located in Chad, Cameroon, Nigeria, and Niger. This lake has slowly been drying up. Once it was one of the largest lakes on the planet, spreading far into what's now the Sahara Desert.

Scientists have discovered that this body of water, called Lake Mega-Chad, covered more than 150,000 square miles. (That's the size of the state of Montana!) It was home to millions of fish and

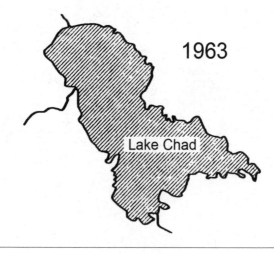

1963

Lake Chad

other animals. But about five thousand years ago, the lake started to dry up and shrink. The lake continues to shrink, and now only covers less than 580 square miles. It is believed that this once gigantic lake could eventually disappear.

As the lake shrinks, the desert takes over. That means it's getting more difficult for people in the area to make a living through farming and fishing. The United Nations says that over ten million people that live around Lake Chad need help to survive.

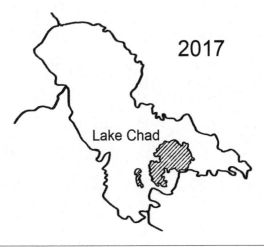

The Ounianga lakes are fed by aquifers (say: a-kwuh-fers). Aquifers are areas of rock below ground that act like sponges. All the cracks, crevices, and spaces between the particles of rock are full of water. The water is able to move up through the layers of rock to the surface. Even though the lake water evaporates quickly due to the heat in the desert, the aquifer is large enough to keep the lakes supplied with water.

Wadis (say: WAH-dees) are ravines or gullies that are dry for most of the year. However, they come to life when it rains. Because the ground is so dry and packed, it doesn't absorb the rain, and the wadis fill up with water and become rivers. But these rivers don't last for a very long time. They disappear quickly because the water evaporates rapidly. Wadis can range in size from a small gully to a deep canyon. Most of the trees and sizable bushes in the Sahara are found near wadis.

A dry wadi

An oasis is a place in a desert where water comes up to the surface from deep underground. It is almost like a reverse island. It is an area of water that is surrounded by an ocean of sand and rock. An oasis can vary in size from just a small grove of trees around a well to a city and the crops that surround it. Oases (the plural of oasis) cover only about eight hundred square miles of the Sahara Desert. And about 75 percent of the people who live in the desert live in or near these oases.

Although an oasis is surrounded by dry, parched ground, the land directly around it is fertile. Trees and other plants, such as figs, wheat, and citrus fruits, are often found near an oasis. And animals that live in the desert come to an oasis to drink, find shade, and graze on the plants.

Mysterious Mirages

There are many stories about thirsty travelers crossing the desert who suddenly see a mirage of an oasis. The traveler runs toward the oasis and tries to jump into the cool water. But just then the oasis disappears, and the traveler is still surrounded by hot, burning sand.

Mirages are caused by layers of air being

different temperatures and different thicknesses. These differences cause light to bend. This bending, called refraction, causes images to appear. They may look very real, but they aren't real at all.

One of the most common examples of a mirage happens on roads and highways in the summer. It often looks like there is a puddle or pool of water on the road up ahead. In the desert, the light refracted from the blue sky looks like water in the sand.

When an oasis is found, people usually plant trees and bushes around it to protect it from the blowing sand. People who travel across the Sahara usually travel from one oasis to another on their journey. The distance between oases might be many, many miles.

CHAPTER 4
Desert Dwellers

Thousands of years ago, when the Sahara was green, many groups of people lived there. Most were nomads, which means they moved from one area to another in search of food and water. Although these groups lived separately from one another, they often traded goods as they traveled across the desert.

But when the green landscape began to transform into desert about four thousand years ago, most of these people moved out. They headed north toward the Mediterranean Sea. They also made their way toward other sources of water, such as Lake Chad and the Nile and Niger Rivers. These people established towns, cities, and eventually empires, including the kingdoms

of ancient Egypt, Ghana, and Mali. The people
who stayed in the desert remained nomadic. They
traveled from oasis to oasis, setting up trade routes
across the desert.

A group of people commonly called the Berbers became the largest group of nomadic people to live in the Sahara. The word "Berber" is thought to have come from an Arabic word for "outsider." That word was adapted from the Greek term "barbaros." The ancient Greeks used this term to describe anyone who didn't speak Greek. However, back then and now, the people of this group refer to themselves as Amazigh, or "free people."

Amazigh people

Over the centuries, the Imazighen (the plural of "Amazigh") faced many invaders, including the ancient Greeks and Romans. Arab armies also moved across northern Africa in the seventh century, vastly outnumbering the Imazighen. Arabs came from the Arabian Peninsula; they were Muslims and followers of the Prophet Muhammad. Many Imazighen converted to Islam, began speaking Arabic, and took on many Arab customs.

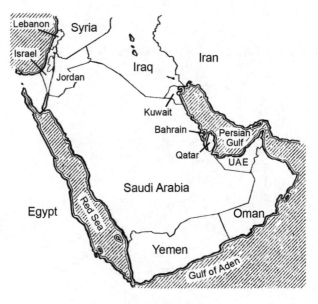

Arabian Peninsula

Islam

Founded by the Prophet Muhammad, Islam is one of the world's major religions. (A prophet is a person believed to be chosen by God to say the things that God wants to tell people.) Its followers are called Muslims. Most Muslims live in Africa, the Middle East, and central and south Asia, but Islam is practiced around the world.

Muslims believe in one god, called Allah, and their holy book is called the Quran (say: ka-rahn). According to Muslims, in 610 CE an angel told Muhammad that Allah had chosen him as a prophet. During the 600s and 700s, as Arabs conquered lands around them, Islam spread. Today about 1.8 billion people are Muslim.

Once the Arabs arrived, some Imazighen gave up their nomadic lifestyle and settled in villages and towns. But many continued to live as nomads in the Sahara Desert. To this day, they travel hundreds of miles searching for new grazing land for their herds of goats and camels.

Amazigh society is organized into tribes. Each tribe includes several large family groups. Each tribe has its own chief, and the chief makes decisions, sets laws and rules, and resolves arguments for the tribe. Most nomadic Imazighen live in portable tents, which they set up whenever they find a good grazing spot or an oasis.

Imazighen are known for how well they treat their guests. A guest is anyone who has been given food and water by an Amazigh. And once you are a guest, they take responsibility for your safety.

The most well-known group of Imazighen in the Sahara Desert are the Tuareg (say: twaa-reg). The Tuareg live in Algeria, Mali, Libya, Burkina

Faso, and Niger, where they raise cows, camels, goats, and chickens. They are also known as the "blue men" because of the blue veils the men wear. The blue dye used to color the veils often rubs off on the men's skin, making it look blue.

It is believed that Tuareg men began wearing these veils to protect themselves from the sand blowing across the desert. The veil is wrapped around their head, with only their eyes showing.

Tuareg woman

Tuareg men who live and work in the desert still often wear a veil, called a tagelmust. However, many of those who have moved to towns and cities no longer wear veils. And it is only Tuareg men who wear these blue veils. Tuareg women do not wear them.

Today, two and a half million people live in the Sahara Desert. That's less than one person per square mile! Most of these people have Amazigh or Arab roots. Tuaregs are a mix of people who live in permanent settlements near sources of water, people who move from place to place as the seasons change, and people who continue to live as nomads and follow ancient trade routes.

CHAPTER 5
Across the Sea of Sand

For hundreds of years, traveling across the Sahara Desert was the way to go for merchants looking to make money. Large groups of traders traveled back and forth across the desert with their goods packed on camels, bringing valuable items from one place to another. Just like the oceans of the world had busy trade routes and bustling ports, so did the Sahara.

Known as the trans-Saharan trade routes, they have existed for thousands of years. People carried goods from west and central Africa, across the vast desert, to the ports on the Mediterranean Sea.

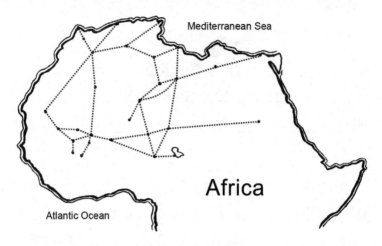

Mediterranean Sea

Africa

Atlantic Ocean

Trans-Saharan trade routes

From there the goods were sent to distant places like the Middle East, Europe, and India. The main items traded were gold and salt. But things such as ivory, shells, cloth, metal, and beads were also exchanged. The trade routes also made it

possible for silk and other cloth from the Middle East, Europe, and India to be transported into Africa.

Historians know that copper from Mauritania in western Africa found its way to people living on the coast of the Mediterranean Sea during the Bronze Age. The Bronze Age was a period in history, from about 3300 BCE to 1200 BCE, when people first started making tools and weapons out of metals, including bronze. (Bronze is made from combining copper and tin.)

Copper

Over the centuries, more and more traders carried goods across the desert. By about the fifth century CE, Imazighen in North Africa had established routes across the desert using camels. They traveled across the Sahara to trade salt, weapons, glassware, and books to people living in the south and west. Some Imazighen also traded enslaved people. In exchange, they received gold, textiles, and ivory.

Because camels were so well adapted to life in the desert, they transported the goods along the trade routes. The long distances, harsh climate, and bandits made the journey dangerous, so it was safer to travel in large groups. These large groups were called caravans. A normal-size caravan might have had one thousand camels, but some caravans had as many as ten thousand camels.

As the trade routes were developed across Africa, towns and cities sprang up along the way. In western Africa, the major trade centers were Timbuktu, Gao, and Djenne. In North Africa, there were the cities of Cairo, Tunis, and Marrakesh.

Trading by crossing the Sahara Desert continued to grow for the next several centuries. It reached its peak during the height of the Mali

Empire in the 1300s. It then began declining in the fifteenth and sixteenth centuries.

Why?

During that period, the Portuguese made advances in seafaring. With their ships they were able to reach the west coast of Africa, and began to colonize this region. They no longer needed to travel across the desert to find natural resources and trade goods. This opened up new routes for trade between Europe and West Africa.

The Mali Empire

Musa

The Mali Empire in West Africa lasted from the 1200s to the 1500s. It grew from a small kingdom on the Niger River to a large empire. The area had an abundance of salt and gold mines, and through trading those resources, the kingdom grew very wealthy.

The most famous Mali emperor was named Musa. He came to the throne around 1307. He expanded the kingdom and made it a powerful center of culture and politics. Musa also made the region a center of Islamic culture and thought.

The Mali Empire began to decline in the 1400s. Many cities were attacked by neighboring people. Also, citizens of some cities rebelled against their own rulers. By 1550, the empire had lost most of its power. Although the kingdom eventually fell, the name "Mali" is still used by the modern country of Mali.

CHAPTER 6
Early Explorers

The Sahara Desert is often called *El Khela*, which means "the emptiness." And this emptiness has fascinated people for thousands of years. But while it has captured people's imaginations, for a long time no one really explored it. The harsh climate, miles of shifting sand, and lack of water were a barrier to exploration. Because of that, not much was known about the Sahara Desert until recently.

The ancient Egyptians lived on the edge of the Sahara Desert. But they only used it as a source of natural resources. Herodotus, an ancient Greek writer, claimed that the continent of Africa ended after the desert.

Records from the ancient Romans show

several expeditions to the Sahara Desert between 19 BCE and 86 CE. Most were searches for valuable natural resources, such as gold and spices. There are also records of the Imazighen traveling across the Sahara Desert in the fifth century as they set up their trade routes.

Herodotus

Ibn Battuta

Ibn Battuta (say: ib-in bah-too-tah) was one of the greatest travelers in history. He explored regions in the western Sahara in the 1300s. He described what he saw in a book he wrote about his adventures.

Ibn Battuta's book

In the 1400s, the Portuguese began exploring Africa, but they limited their journeys to the west and east coasts of the continent. They didn't travel inland. After that, there was little exploration by Europeans until the 1700s.

In 1795, Mungo Park, a doctor from Scotland, was hired by the African Association to explore the Niger River. The African Association had been founded in England in 1788. Its mission was to find the source of the Niger River and the location of Timbuktu, "the lost city of gold." But imprisonment by a local chief, illness, and a lack of supplies brought an end to Park's expedition.

However, Park wrote about his travels. The book came out in 1797 and made Park famous. Several years later, the African Association asked him to lead another expedition to western Africa. In 1805, Park and his traveling companions made their way from present-day Gambia to the Niger River, with many dying from illness. But at the Bussa Rapids, the men were attacked by locals, and Park drowned while trying to escape.

Mungo Park

Timbuktu

Timbuktu (say: tim-buck-too) is a city in Mali. People will often use the name to describe a place that is very far away and almost unreachable. The city was founded in the twelfth century by Tuareg nomads. Within two hundred years, it had become a very wealthy city. It was at the center of several important trading routes across the Sahara. Descriptions of this rich city reached Europe and captured the imagination of Europeans. But because of its location in the Sahara Desert, it was extremely difficult to reach. It remained unknown to foreigners for hundreds of years.

Friedrich Hornemann

In 1798, a German explorer named Friedrich Hornemann joined a caravan heading across the northeastern part of the Sahara. He was the first European to cross this part of the desert, and he gathered a lot of information about the region's geography and the people who lived there. Hornemann sent his journals to London and they were published in 1802. However, he never returned to Europe and it's not known what happened to him.

In 1824, the Geographical Society of Paris announced it would award a large monetary prize to the first European to return alive from Timbuktu. In July 1825, the Scottish explorer Alexander Gordon Laing set off from Tripoli (in present-day Libya) with a group of men in search of the mysterious city. But in January 1826, Laing and his party were attacked by a band of Tuareg.

Most of his party was killed, and Laing was severely injured. Despite this, he joined a caravan, which did reach Timbuktu in August 1826. Laing wrote a letter on September 21, 1826, saying that staying in Timbuktu was difficult and that he intended to leave. He did start back but was killed in the desert five days later.

René-Auguste Caillié was born into a poor family in France. Before he even turned twenty years old, he had made two trips into present-day Senegal. To prepare for his journey to Timbuktu, Caillié studied Arabic and Islamic beliefs. In April 1827, he disguised himself as a Muslim pilgrim and set off from present-day Sierra Leone on his expedition to Timbuktu. Caillié joined a caravan and arrived in the city a year later. Upon his return to France, the Geographical Society of Paris awarded him the prize. Caillié wrote about his travels, which were published in 1830. However, he never went on another expedition.

René-Auguste Caillié

Several other expeditions into the Sahara were made by German and French explorers through the 1800s. By the end of the nineteenth century, the main features of the Sahara were known. Nevertheless, in 1922, an Egyptian named Ahmed Hassanein set off across the eastern part of the Sahara Desert. He hoped to make further discoveries. His journey took eight months. He traveled 2,200 miles by camel and on foot.

What he saw led to corrections on earlier maps of the desert. He also discovered the famous petroglyphs of Uweinat in Egypt.

Ahmed Hassanein

Even today, the lure of the Sahara draws travelers on expeditions into its miles and miles of sand and rock.

Alexandrine Tinné

In the nineteenth century, many young women went on "grand tours" of Europe. But that sounded a bit boring to Alexandrine Tinné. She wanted to go on a much bigger adventure. Tinné, who was

Dutch, had been fascinated by Africa since she was a little girl. So when her father passed away and left her a large fortune, she decided to use it to explore that continent.

In 1869, she hoped to be the first European woman to cross the Sahara. She brought two iron tanks filled with water on the expedition. It is believed by some that local people spread rumors that the tanks were actually filled with gold coins. Her party was attacked and Tinné was killed. She didn't achieve her goal of crossing the Sahara, but she did collect a lot of information about the region. Tinné and her colleagues took photographs of plants and animals that were unknown to the European world at the time. They also collected specimens of their discoveries and sent them back to Europe.

CHAPTER 7
Creatures of the Sahara

Though they may not always be visible, the desert is full of unusual plants and animals. Life in the Sahara is a challenge. But the plants and animals here have found ways to endure the lack of water, hot temperatures during the day, and cool temperatures at night.

More than five hundred species of plant live in the Sahara Desert. (A species is a group of animals, plants, or other living things that all share common characteristics.) Grasses and herbs grow in the very driest places. However, little else can survive in those

Date palm

areas. Most other plant species, such as acacia trees, tamarisk bushes, and date palms, are found along the northern and southern edges of the desert and near oases.

Tamarisk bush

Many of the plants in the Sahara have developed long roots. These long roots are able to reach the water in the aquifers that lie beneath the sand. The roots of some plants may grow to around eighty feet long. (That's about twice the height of a telephone pole!) The trees in the desert usually have thick bark and waxy leaves, which helps them conserve and store water.

Acacia tree

Even though it doesn't rain often in the Sahara Desert, flowering plants make the most of this moisture. After it rains, these plants complete their growing cycle quickly. They put down shallow roots to capture the moisture and produce seeds before the soil dries out. The new seeds may lie dormant, or not active, in the dry ground for years. They wait for the next rainfall so that the flowering plant can repeat this cycle.

The Amazing Acacia Tree

The acacia tree is one of the few species of trees that can survive in the heat and arid conditions of the Sahara Desert. And it is important to the ecosystem and to the people who live there. (An ecosystem is a specific area where living and nonliving things interact and work together as a unit.) The leaves are a source of food for insects and grazing herds of animals. Birds nest in its branches. The resin, or sap, is used as an ointment to treat wounds. And the wood from the tree is used as fuel.

The shape of the acacia tree is very recognizable. The branches spread out like an umbrella, and this makes the trees easy to spot in the desert. One of the most famous acacia trees in the Sahara Desert was the Tree of Ténéré. For hundreds of years, it was the only tree for 250 miles in Niger's area of the Sahara. It was one of the only visible landmarks in that great stretch of sand. Almost all maps of the area showed the tree. Because the tree had survived so long, many people considered it sacred.

Sadly, in 1973, a truck driver who was traveling across the desert hit the tree and killed it. What was left of the tree was taken to the Niger National Museum, and a sculpture was erected where the tree had stood.

Remains of the Tree of Ténéré

About seventy species of mammals, ninety species of birds, one hundred species of reptiles  and amphibians, plus several species of scorpions, spiders, and other small arthropods live in the Sahara. (An arthropod is a creature that has a hard shell on the outside of its body, jointed legs, and no bones.) All have adapted special ways to cope with the harsh conditions of the desert. Many are nocturnal, which means they are active at night, when the desert is cooler.

The fennec fox is one of these animals. It is the smallest fox in the world. Its large ears help release heat from its body and keep it cool. These large ears also pick up even the faintest sounds of prey as the fennec fox hunts at night. And its furry feet protect the fox from the burning desert sand.

Other animals that you may spot in the desert are baboons, gazelles, hyenas, hedgehogs, and jerboas.

The birds that live in the Sahara range from some of the smallest to some of the largest in the world. Many species of bird cross the Sahara as they migrate from one region of the world to the other. The largest bird in the world, the ostrich, can be found in the Sahara. Ostriches are nomads and move around in search of food and water.

They have long eyelashes that protect their eyes from the blowing sand. And their downy feathers create a kind of insulation from the scorching temperatures.

The addax is a type of large antelope that has long, corkscrew-shaped horns. They are one of the few species of antelope where males and females have horns of the same length. Large herds of this animal were once found all across North Africa. But due to overhunting, the species became threatened with extinction. It is believed that fewer than five hundred of these antelope remain in the wild.

The most recognizable animal that lives in the Sahara Desert is the dromedary, or Arabian camel. These camels used to be wild, but they were domesticated about three to four thousand years ago. (A domesticated animal is one that has been tamed and is kept by humans.) Camels are perfectly suited to life in the harsh desert climate. They can survive for long periods without food or water. That is because they store fat, which is used as a source of energy, in their hump. Camels can easily carry a load of two hundred pounds and walk about twenty miles a day. They have two rows of thick eyelashes and can squeeze their nostrils shut. These traits help protect their eyes and noses from blowing sand. Because they are so well suited to this harsh life and carry cargo across the Sahara, camels are known as "ships of the desert."

It's hard to imagine that frogs, toads, and crocodiles live in a desert. But these creatures make their homes in the lakes and oases of the Sahara. They find shelter in caves and dens if  the water dries up. The Sahara frog is very adaptable. It can be found wherever there is water in this desert, from oases to irrigation canals. Sahara frogs can grow up to four inches in length. They can be green or brown or a mixture of those colors, and they usually have spots on their legs.

Snakes, lizards, spiders, and scorpions burrow into the sand and between rocks. This helps them stay cool while they keep an eye out for prey and avoid predators. The deathstalker scorpion is thought to be one of the most dangerous species of scorpion. Its venom is extremely poisonous, and a sting from one of these scorpions can kill you. But this scorpion also helps save lives. Its venom is used to help treat certain kinds of cancer.

One Hump or Two?

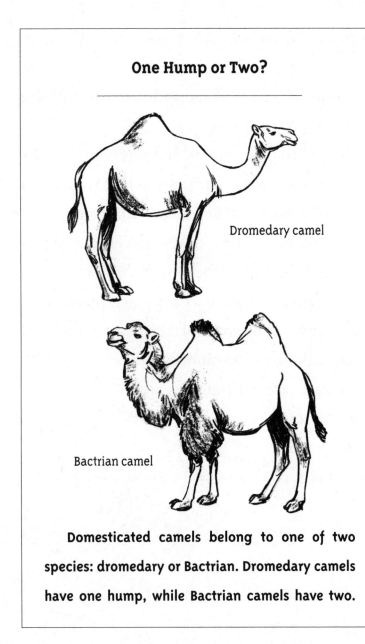

Dromedary camel

Bactrian camel

Domesticated camels belong to one of two species: dromedary or Bactrian. Dromedary camels have one hump, while Bactrian camels have two.

Dromedary camels come from the Arabian Peninsula, and Bactrian camels come from central and east Asia. Both species of camel have been domesticated and used as working animals for thousands of years, with dromedary camels being used on trade routes in the Sahara. Bactrian camels are usually larger than dromedary camels, and they are also able to withstand colder temperatures. They are used in the Gobi Desert in Asia, where it can be as cold as minus forty degrees Fahrenheit in the winter. Because of this, Bactrian camels have long, shaggy coats that help keep them warm. They shed this long coat in the summer months when the desert gets hot.

Dromedary camels greatly outnumber Bactrian camels. Scientists believe there are about two million domesticated Bactrian camels in the world—but there are over fourteen million dromedary camels on the planet.

CHAPTER 8
A Desert at Risk

Although the Sahara is thousands of years old, it is a fragile environment that is constantly under threat. Scientists and organizations around the world have come to realize that this unique area, and all the things that live within it, need to be protected.

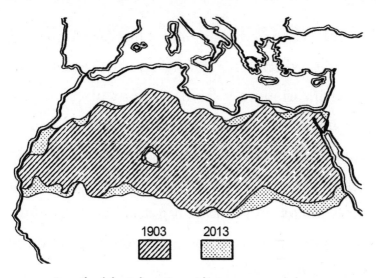

Growth of the Sahara Desert between 1903 and 2013

The biggest threat to the Sahara is desertification. Desertification occurs when the desert begins to take over parts of the land around it that were once fertile. Every year, the Sahara Desert gets a bit bigger. It is estimated to grow at least three to six miles each year. This huge desert is 10 percent bigger than it was just one hundred years ago. As the desert gets bigger, it means that the area where people live, grow crops, and raise animals gets smaller.

All the deserts on our planet are impacted by desertification. However, the causes of desertification vary from place to place. In the Sahara, desertification is caused by natural events, climate change, and human activities. The wind that sweeps across the Sahara blows sand into areas where it is not usually found. As the amount of sand in these areas increases, so does the size of the desert.

The earth's climate has always changed, depending on how much of the sun's energy is absorbed by the atmosphere. Over the past 650,000 years, the climate on our planet has gone through seven ice ages and warming periods. But recently, human activity is having an impact on how quickly and extremely the climate is changing.

Certain gases in the earth's atmosphere, including carbon dioxide, block heat from escaping. The same way that glass roofs and walls in a greenhouse keep plants warm, these gases help keep the earth warm. For the past few hundred years, humans have relied on coal, oil, and gas to power factories, homes, and cars. These sources of energy release carbon dioxide into the atmosphere. This extra carbon dioxide traps more heat in the atmosphere. More heat in the atmosphere increases the earth's temperature and warms up our planet. And a warmer planet is a threat to all life on Earth.

Climate change impacts the weather around the world. It makes wet places wetter and dry places drier. And this change is happening at a very fast pace. So even though the Sahara is getting larger due to natural causes, climate change is speeding up that process.

The Sahel region that borders the Sahara in the south is thought to be experiencing the most desertification in Africa. In this area, human

activity, combined with severe drought, is the biggest cause of desertification. Trees that border the desert are being cut down, and the wood is used as fuel or sold. Farmers are letting their animals graze in the same area too often and too long. This practice, called overgrazing, makes it difficult for plants to grow back. Without trees and plants to hold the moisture and soil in place, the ground dries out and soon becomes desert.

Help for the Sahara

The Sahara Conservation Fund (or SCF) was established in 2004. At that time, many species in the region, such as the addax antelope, were threatened by extinction due to overhunting. The SCF is dedicated to conserving the wildlife, habitats, and other natural resources of the Sahara and the grasslands of the Sahel. The SCF works with governments, scientific organizations, zoos, and international associations to protect this fragile area and the animals and plants that live there.

The United Nations (called the UN for short) is an organization formed to help solve problems around the world. It declared 2006 the International Year of Deserts and Desertification. The organization's mission was to bring attention to the world's deserts and the problem of desertification. Throughout that year, the UN celebrated the importance of all the deserts on the planet. It worked to show the diversity of the people, plants, and animals living in these regions. The goal was to help the world understand that these areas on the planet need to be preserved and protected. The program was so successful that the UN created the Decade for Deserts and the Fight Against Desertification, which ran from January 2010 to December 2020.

CHAPTER 9
A Trip Across the Sahara

A lot of people visit the Sahara Desert every year. Biologists and zoologists go to study the environment. Archaeologists hope to find out

more about the people who lived in the Sahara thousands of years ago. And paleontologists dig for fossils to better understand what life was like in the region millions of years ago.

But scientists aren't the only people who visit the Sahara Desert. It's an incredible place for tourists to visit, and it's now easier than ever to travel there. But the more people who visit the

Sahara, the more likely it is that the desert will be harmed or destroyed.

So if you do get a chance to visit the Sahara Desert, you should be an ecotourist. As an ecotourist, you are mindful about the environment, and the plants, animals, and people that live there. You look to stay in hotels, take tours, and buy souvenirs that don't harm the

Ouarzazate, Morocco

environment and instead support the local community. It's a fantastic way to see the unique places on the planet and help preserve and protect them at the same time.

What would a trip be like?

You might start your trip in Marrakesh, a city in western Morocco. From Marrakesh, a drive to the town of Ouarzazate (say: wear-zeh-zet) would take you over the Atlas Mountains. On the drive through these desert mountains, you would pass through Amazigh villages. In Ouarzazate, you could visit the Noor Ouarzazate Solar Complex, one of the largest solar power plants in the world.

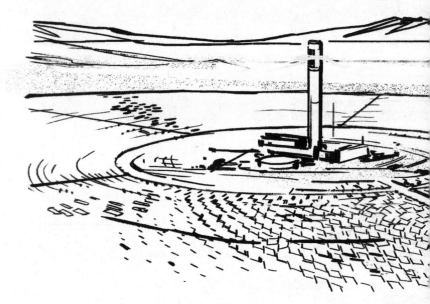

This is a perfect place for a solar power plant, as this region receives some of the highest amounts of sunlight on the planet.

From Ouarzazate, you might travel southeast to the Draa Valley and then on to the village of Tafraoute Sidi Ali. It's now time to get on a camel and join a caravan! From Tafraoute Sidi Ali you would travel through Erg Chebbi,

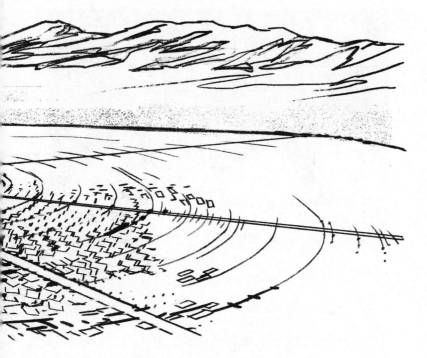

Noor Ouarzazate Solar Complex

one of the largest areas of sand dunes, or ergs, in Morocco. The dunes stretch over thirteen miles in length and three miles in width, and they can reach heights of five hundred feet. You'll camp in the desert tonight and need to wrap up warm as it will get pretty cold. And don't forget to look up at the night sky. It will be filled with more stars than you've ever seen!

After your night in the desert, it's back on the camel and time to head to Merzouga. This village was once used as a stopping place by traders traveling to and from Timbuktu. Merzouga is on the edge of Erg Chebbi, close to Algeria's border. From Merzouga it's time to travel back over the Atlas Mountains to Marrakesh. It's been an extraordinary journey through this unique part of the world. And you can always come back and see more of the millions of square miles that make up the Sahara Desert.

Timeline of the Sahara Desert

c. 2000 BCE	The Sahara transforms from a wet to dry climate
19 BCE– 86 CE	Ancient Romans make several expeditions into the Sahara
c. 400 CE	Imazighen have established trade routes across the Sahara
1300s	Height of the kingdom of Mali in West Africa
1400s	Portuguese begin exploring the west coast of Africa
1798	Friedrich Hornemann is the first European to cross northeastern region of the Sahara
1800s	European countries begin to colonize areas of Africa
1826	Alexander Gordon Laing is the first European to reach Timbuktu, dies on return trip
1828	René-Auguste Caillié is the first European to return from a trip to Timbuktu
1955	A civil war begins in Sudan
1962	Algeria gains independence from France
2001	The first Festival in the Desert is held in Mali
2019	Stone structures, thousands of years old, discovered in western Sahara
2020	Fossils of huge aquatic dinosaur found in Morocco

Timeline of the World

c. 9500 BCE —	The last ice age ends
27 BCE —	Start of the Roman Empire
250–900 CE —	Height of the Maya Empire
1095 —	Start of the Crusades
1488 —	Portuguese explorer Bartolomeu Dias sails around the Cape of Good Hope
1666 —	The Great Fire of London occurs
1789 —	French Revolution begins
1841 —	British biologist Richard Owen uses the word "dinosaur" for the first time
1876 —	Alexander Graham Bell is granted a patent for the telephone
1918 —	Spanish flu pandemic begins
1969 —	Neil Armstrong becomes the first person to walk on the moon
1994 —	Nelson Mandela elected president of South Africa
2020 —	Joe Biden elected as the forty-sixth president of the United States

Bibliography

*Books for young readers

*Aloian, Molly. ***The Sahara Desert***. Deserts Around the World. New York: Crabtree, 2012.

De Villiers, Marq, and Sheila Hirtle. ***Sahara: The Extraordinary History of the World's Largest Desert***. New York: Walker, 2002.

Gardi, René. ***Sahara***. Bern, Switzerland: Kümmerly & Frey, 1970.

Gearon, Eamonn. ***The Sahara: A Cultural History***. Oxford, England: Oxford University Press, 2011.

*Lappi, Megan. ***The Sahara Desert: The Largest Desert in the World***. Natural Wonders. New York: Weigl Publishers, 2007.

Norwich, John Julius. ***Sahara***. New York: Weybright and Talley, 1968.

*Rector, Rebecca Kraft. ***The Sahara Desert***. Natural Wonders of the World. Lake Elmo, MN: Focus Readers, 2018.

*Weintraub, Aileen. ***The Sahara Desert: The Biggest Desert***. Great Record Breakers in Nature. New York: Rosen Publishing Group, 2001.

Williams, Martin. ***When the Sahara Was Green: How Our Greatest Desert Came to Be***. Princeton, NJ: Princeton University Press, 2021.